THE GOODBYE WORLD POEM

BRIAN TURNER

ALICE JAMES BOOKS
New Gloucester, ME
alicejamesbooks.org

CELEBRATING 50 YEARS
OF ALICE JAMES BOOKS

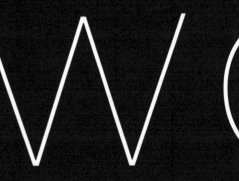

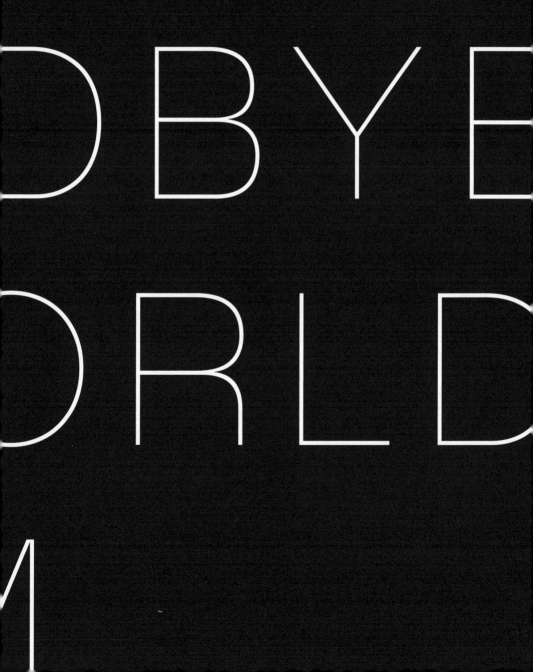

10 9 8 7 6 5 4 3 2 1

Alice James Books are published by Alice James Poetry Cooperative, Inc.

Alice James Books
Auburn Hall
60 Pineland Drive, Suite 206
New Gloucester, ME 04260
www.alicejamesbooks.org

Library of Congress Cataloging-in-Publication Data

Names: Turner, Brian, 1967- author.
Title: The goodbye world poem / Brian Turner.
Description: New Gloucester, ME : Alice James Books, 2023
Identifiers: LCCN 2023018347 (print) | LCCN 2023018348 (ebook)
  ISBN 9781949944549 (trade paperback) | ISBN 9781949944280 (epub)
Subjects: LCSH: Grief—Poetry. | Death—Poetry. | Memory—Poetry. | LCGFT: Poetry.
Classification: LCC PS3620.U763 G66 2023 (print) | LCC PS3620.U763 (ebook)
  DDC 811/.6—dc23/eng/20230504
LC record available at https://lccn.loc.gov/2023018347
LC ebook record available at https://lccn.loc.gov/2023018348

Alice James Books gratefully acknowledges support from individual donors, private
foundations, the National Endowment for the Arts, and the Amazon Literary Partnership.

Cover Photo: Self Reflected Sunburst, reflective microetching under multicolored light.
2014–2021, Greg Dunn and Brian Edwards

CONTENTS

—PREFACE—

My love, last night
I woke from a dream in which light
dripped from your fingers, your hair,
and you cupped it in your palms,
saying, *Love, this is for you.*
All of this is yours.

What does one do with such a gift?

THE CROSSING

There's always a ship on fire, the whole thing
listing to starboard and falling to pieces with flames
in the sailcloth and rigging, the vessel disappearing
into dusk, into the blue and widening universe.
That's how all the stories end, with a film score
calling for a *crescendo*, followed by a *diminuendo*.
The tempo marked *grave*. Twenty-five to forty-five
beats per minute. As it is with the human heart
at the close of day. *Larghetto* to *lento* to *largo*
to *grave*. The body winding down.

Is it wrong to think of it, dying, as beautiful?

It feels wrong in my own body. When I say it
out loud. When I imagine not a ship on fire
but Ilyse in our bedroom, that Tuesday morning
in September. A fever spiking in her the night
before, how we tore the bath towels to shreds,
dunked them into a bucket of ice water, then
draped them over her arms and legs, stomach
and chest, the smooth dome of her shaved head.
I leaned in close to blow softly on her wet skin.

Dying is so intimate.

Candlelight flickered under the Buddha's gaze.
Even the words spoken by the hospice nurse

vanished into air. A warm scent of lavender
drifted from one hour to another. And as the heat
crested within her, then eased, I lay down beside her
to have one last conversation about this world,
to revel in all that she'd created here, revisiting
the path she'd traveled, reciting her verses
one by one, saying, *I love you, I love you, I love you.*

AND THEN THE SILENCE.

And the palm trees swaying in the sun,
their pleated shadows brushing the concrete
as if inscribing it with a language that recedes
hour by hour, month by month, though the trees
keep trying. As it was with the caregivers at home.
Those hard metal wheels rolling on a wooden floor.
Everything fallen into a hush, as it should be.
As it was with family. Friends. Flowers at the door.
Envelopes sealed with a cursive of mourning.
The mouths of strangers opening and
closing as if all the world were submerged with me
in this quiet place I'm learning is the rest of my life.

29 DOWN, 14 ACROSS

How alive the dead appear in the moment
after. In the hush and stillness of the body.
Their lips so soft, their closed eyes deep
in the enormous task a lifetime of dreaming
asks of them. Why has it taken these last goodbyes
for me to attend to the sacred in those I love?
I think of Ilyse's laughter, the warmth
of her palm resting on my thigh, the silent
conversations she held with the ocean.
And when cancer broke her vertebrae,
she leaned her head back to exhale
a pluming column of smoke, her pain
beyond anything I've ever experienced,
and yet, the expression on her face then,
that release, her hands riding the air,
a pair of birds in tandem flight.
I have these to look back on. More.
Flashes of light. Fragments. Some
of what the vault of the mind offers up.
But what of the gaps in memory? Each
quiet erasure occurring inside of us.
If only I'd been more aware, more alive,
I could stretch out on the couch with my head
in her lap again, listening to her breathe
as she focuses on a crossword puzzle, her mind
wandering through the passages of her life—
opening doors, opening books, listening to music

until, once again, she arrives at the answers
to 29 Down, 14 Across, the ballpoint
pressing ink into each square, letter by letter,
her free hand caressing my face,
her fingertips, little fireworks.

HANAUMA BAY

—*Springtime, 2015*

In another version of this life, the pull of the outgoing tide
was simply too strong, and no matter how hard my legs kicked
the adrenaline turned to panic in the muscle, the figures
on the shoreline receding, as in a painting, the water
brushed smooth with phthalo-blue given veins of salt,
the hills beyond daubed with the green flames of trees
as Ilyse, her voice too distant to hear, could only watch
as I was swept out to sea, my remains never recovered,
though a humpback breached the mouth of the harbor then
to turn in a slow corkscrew of air, the whale suspended
between ocean and sky, as if it meant to spy into the deep
for a dead swimmer in the current, to glimpse sight of me,
my body, no longer driven by oxygen or sunlight, now
tumbling and turning, my arms reaching back toward
all I'd ever known, my torso curling into a question, limbs
a blur of motion as my body began to tangle and spin—
a dance witnessed by triggerfish and surgeonfish, green
sea turtles gliding alongside me, solemn as undertakers
in search of the shadowy wings of manta rays, those flyers
who would guide me into all that is cold and absolute.

VIGIL

When I think of my father in the ICU, intubated,
with whole decades of our lives tunneling in
as I tried to give voice to the last words
ever, and the language failed me, completely,
it's his expression that comes to mind—
such tenderness, such compassion.
There is so much my eyes have seen,
that my hands have done, and yet
I know almost nothing. How many losses
will it take for something like wisdom to set in?
How many doorways into the sublime need to open
for me to fully inhabit the wider landscape
of the soul? There is no false humility in this, just
one human being looking inward and remembering
my brother's voice on the phone, that last call
after a year of chemo and the doctor's death sentence
coming due, my brother saying, *You don't even know*
how good a glass of water tastes. And of course
he's right. I light the candles as each anniversary
arrives. For Ilyse. For my father. For my brother.
Votive candles for uncles, grandparents, friends
long gone. Each an act of memory. Devotion. Lament.
I watch these figures move under the Buddha's statue,
how they sway to the teardrop of light pooling
in a well of beeswax. Do they band around me
to summon and relive their time on Earth,
or are they here to help me on my way, in this

slow crossing of mine, the small deaths I usher in
each day, as the dead whisper all that must be done,
gesturing me toward them, saying, *It's okay. It's alright.*
There is no dying of the light, there is only this
shimmering dusk, this gathering of souls
into the deep shadow of a mountain.

THE DEAD GUYS

Ghosts? Oh, I've got ghosts. They visit on the porch
sometimes when the wind blows through, chimes
ringing in the trees. My brother describes the fentanyl
and pancreatic cancer in his veins, that cold blueing
of the pistol in Johnny's mouth. This is Fresno
he's telling me about. Home. Where the fog rolls over
the San Joaquin Valley. He says something about the one
he loved, long gone now, the one who moved to Ohio
because he just never could say the words out loud,
the most important things. A sad kind of gift
from the father to the son. He tells me he's sorry
about all that happened to Uncle Paul,
how his body fell apart in equal measure
to the way his life fell apart. As it is for many.
And Pleshy. Remember him? How he shot himself
in the face, but didn't die, just moaning in the yard
with his blown-off jaw, bleeding in the dirt.
These things we do to ourselves, my brother says.
These things we do to each other. Remember
how we drove each dream into the ground, crushing
cross-tops and snorting them off the hood, then
smoking weed at dawn to bring ourselves down?
Remember the LSD, the mushrooms, crystal meth,
that crack pipe, that joint dipped in formaldehyde?
How we survived our twenties I don't have a clue,
though maybe it was the music. Tube amplifiers.
Kick drums. Distortion that brought a new form

of beauty into the world. The set list we played
and repeated until the air itself charged electric,
A minor/ D minor/ G, B minor at the bridge,
our bodies humming a new vocabulary we swore
to honor with our lives. *Remember that*, he says.
And of course I do. It's all jumbled around inside of me.
The whole city of Fresno. Divisadero Street. Blackstone.
Skinheads with their aluminum bats. Veteranos
with *Bulldogs* tattooed across their necks. Hmong
and Laotian tagged on the fencelines. A police officer
shining a Maglite into my eyes, as if he had any idea
what might be found there, in those widening
pools where the ghosts are, my brother
among them now, saying, *You know, it's not true,*
I told her how much I loved her, all kinds
of ways, all the time, but she left me just the same.

THERA

We were all Jack Gilbert's lovers, not in the world
but in the poems, in the world of the poems, dying
on the rocky broken slopes of hard islands in a blue
country across the sea, lovers carried in his arms
for decades sometimes, more, the wind a character
that refused to lift the center of the word *pain*, where
vowels fall into the letter *n* the way the summer,
wheat-blazed and feral, pours into the cold weeks
of November, winter in its bones to come. Jack
loved us, not as a god or a devil, however nuanced,
but as one who must attend to the difficult harvest
of a life, to the losses and the simple grain that we might,
if we listen beyond the howling in our own hearts, hear
him singing of as he carries us up the dead mountain.

ALL THE QUIET RUIN IN GILBERT'S POEMS

Listen. He's describing all that isn't here. All
that emptiness around us, as well as everything
that remains. Boats appearing off the coastline,
then disappearing. A warm brass of sunlight
curling in the soft metals of her hair.
His hands brush through the air as if
rowing the sculpture of a wave
across the invisible, one after another.

He says, *Love allows us to walk*
in the sweet music of our particular heart.
And what more is there to say?
We spend a lifetime gathering our share
of beauty, pain, suffering, wonder.
Not the branches made still by moonlight,
but the moonlight itself, shaping a world.
Not the cry of a lover in the darkness
but what it takes for lovers to draft
each note, that untangling of desire
so deep within the muscle the body
shudders in waves to release it.

I'm reminded of the curtains glowing
in the tall windows of our apartment
in Delft, a cool breeze lifting and falling
as we lay exhausted in a bed of clouds,
endorphins flooding through us, our tongues

wet with the language of the body. And all of it
gone now, submerged into something as simple
as the word *after*. A word that rises ever so briefly
before diminishing into the letter *r*, as cruel
as that might sound, and just as sweet.

FALLING GIANTS

When a whale dies, its body eventually sinks to the ocean floor, an event
known as a *whale fall*. They fall from one region to another, mile
after mile into the gloom, into the pressures of the fathoms below.
I imagine them falling beyond the continental shelf off California.
The whales fall headfirst, in solitude, and they fall with seamounts cast
as dramatic backdrops in the distance. They fall toward a landscape of karsts,
where deep fissures in the earth vent gasses and wide canyons harbor
entire ecosystems, as if falling toward the cities of the deep.

They plummet through the cold, shredded by seabirds and sharks above,
with the rags of their flesh rippling in the descent, the bloodless flags
of giants whose stature remains true even as the last rays of light cast
upon them, guiding them homeward to their fixed stations on the seabed,
far below, where they feed the beaks of squid and the mouths of worms
year after year, with each whale consumed to its skeletal state,
and all of this before the arrival of boneworms, or zombie worms
as they're known, who disassemble bone with enzymes and acid,
the deconstruction of each whale a journey that requires
a kingdom of sea life on the ocean floor, a process
that lasts at least fifty years, bringing them to completion.

I see the whales as they fall from the lighted world, falling in silence, alone.
They fall from one blue atmosphere into another, and they fall, unrecorded,
through the passages of history. They fall into a hunger they cannot imagine,
with the sound of loved ones in their ears, calling to them, sonorous
and mournful, the pathos undeniable, and mournful because called out

for love's sake, the fluid world a conduit for the voices of these giants, who sound themselves across the globe, across generations, speaking to their loved ones, calling out to each as I watch the whales fall, one after another, until their shadowy forms disappear into the cold.

Their mouths are open, and they breathe in the beautiful dark as they fall. They carry the decades of their lives with them, filled with visions of the gunmetal ocean pounded by thunder, charged with lightning and the midnight voltage of a storm far out at sea. They plummet with their sunken eyes filled with streets of clouds, kelp beds, the harvest of hunger in a school of krill, the quick flight of capelin and mackerel. They fall with memories of those they loved, the sensation of two immense bodies sliding and brushing alongside one another in the deep, the pain and wonder of a newborn calf slipping from within one's body and into a life of its own, and that rush of driving a metallic shoal of fish to the surface in the hunt together, the thrill of breaching the surface to rise into the clear air, that momentary flight into sunlight, that bright suspension, the voices of birds calling out, otherworldly, where they breathe in the oxygen and then carry it down by the lungful into the currents below, holding it inside themselves, pondering over the invisible mystery of it, each breath held for as long as an hour before ascending once more to the surface with a terrific blast of exhalation, a kind of announcement to the universe that they were here, on planet Earth, a presence in this world, *alive*.

IN THIS HOUSE OF FLESH AND BONE

There will be rain in the story.
A series of voices. Birds. Maybe
a character flaw some find charming.
There will be pain, of course,
and laughter. Some small
sweet gesture, like the way
she used to hold my face
in the tender cups of her palms
before kissing me, moments
that gather into something
one might call a life. This
story we tell ourselves
as loved ones cross over
one by one.
                    We are learning
how to care for the dead, each
in our own way. So, too, the living.
We lean our heads back and listen
to music translated from the air
as memory draws our fingers
through a loved one's hair
before brushing the stone
to reveal the pooling shadows
of the chisel.
                    It's something
like prayer, I think, the way others might
talk to god within the vaulted spaces

of the body, one's voice spoken

into the long corridors swept clean

of shadow, there by the opened windows

where the birds might one day

fly in at dawn, singing.

LOS ANGELES

It's one of those things I have little memory of—
my half brother, a toddler, floating facedown
in the pool, his lips turned an awful shade of blue.
Around us, the city slept on. A coastal fog rolled in
as seagulls wheeled above, crying out in hunger.
I'm told I saved him by climbing a flight of stairs
to wake my exhausted young mother, a go-go dancer
at a club in North Hollywood. What I remember
are the Crown Royal bags full of her nightly tips,
the snare drum I'd bang along to Iron Butterfly,
drumming my heart out to that 2 ½-minute solo
on the extended jam of "In-A-Gadda-Da-Vida,"
the Summer of Love playing in the background.
My little brother was raised by his own father
in Buena Park, while our mother returned with me
to the San Joaquin Valley. He lived with us once
for a year, when he was a 6ᵗʰ grader, setting fire
to the dead grasslands around us, stealing a pistol
from the neighbor's house, discharging a shotgun
into the furniture, and chasing Ronald McCree
with a can of hair spray and a lighter improvised
into a blowtorch. The years would not be kind to him.
He spent a couple of them under the California
Youth Authority. Then a series of halfway houses.
A failed marriage. His own kids, my niece and nephews,
doing time now, one of them on the run after an incident
with a weapon and a stolen car. And he's back in Fresno

now, living on the streets, with pills and crystal meth
searing through his veins. And I have to wonder
who is he, this brother of mine. Because that little boy
floating in the pool long ago, he never really made it out,
a part of him died right there in the water, and I didn't
save him at all, and I haven't, to this day, ever really met
the man I call my little brother, that blue-lipped child
who was a toddler when he fell in, only 14 months
younger than me, and what the hell did we know
about water, or air, or drowning, or anything at all.

FEAR

Let me tell you—an inside pitch can alter your life.
   Just ask any hitter with a shattered
jawbone, busted kneecap, or broken knuckles.
   It's been like this throughout the game.
A century ago, with Ray Chapman in the box,
   the submariner for the Yankees, Carl Mays
rocked back, coiling into himself like tempered
   steel, then seemed to scrape the stitched globe
of the ball across the grit of the mound as he threw,
   the way my little brother and I skipped stones
over the moonlit surface of Hensley Lake, or
   out on the gravel drive at home, pitching
flattened stones with a snap and twist so they rose
   in curving arcs that buckled each other's knees
and sent us stumbling back cursing as each stone
   whizzed past. It was a practice in the fundamentals
of fear. A practice I never mastered. Not even close.
   But my little brother, he thrived on it, the years
breaking his teeth, breaking his nose, breaking bones,
   the batter's box become the whole world, the way
he punched a CHP officer in a dirt lot off the freeway
   in Anaheim, the way two men cracked his kneecaps
with a baseball bat in San Jose and he laughed about it

afterward, saying, *What else you gonna do? That all you got?*
As if life were nothing more than a repetition of violence,
    with baseball elevating it all to an art form, a combination
of speed and power and grace, a sport he was good at,
    good enough to play in the minors, maybe,
he was *that* good, but he was better at taking drugs, and still is,
    numbing the pain, I think, separating himself from it
until the fog rolls deep in the San Joaquin Valley, erasing everything.

And I don't know what to make of it all. I can't seem to get the image
    out of my head—as I'm reminded of it with every game I watch.
Maybe it's the same for you. You ever notice how they switch
    the ball—anytime it hits the dirt—to cast out the scuffed
for the new? That's because of what happened to Ray Chapman
    at the Polo Grounds on August 16th, 1920, bottom of the 5th,
when Mays took the sign, then reached down almost as if
    dunking that ball into the midnight waters of Hensley Lake,
the same lake where I would eventually pour the ashes
    of my best friend after a yearlong battle with cancer,
the same waters we'd all fished as kids, lifting the cold bodies
    of catfish and bass from the deep, slick and silver,
their mouths gasping a secret about death, same as the pitch
    rising from the shadows of the mound to stun the batter
and everyone there, the sound of it like the crack of a bat,
    and Chapman, bleeding from his ear, still trying
to get to first base—that's what I think of every time
    the catcher swaps the ball with the umpire, a new ball
brought into the game. I'm thinking of Chapman dying,
    the only player ever killed by the game, though
I know that's not true. Because I'm thinking of my brother
    in that burnt summer field, the officers gathered round
to beat him down, the men in San Jose swinging aluminum

in the night, the way he never steps out of the box,
the way he always leans in, the way he cocks his head,

    waiting for it, waiting for the hardest pitch I can throw
from childhood, where we studied it, where we learned it all.

THE CARE UNIT SOFTBALL TEAM

Before we could head over to the park to take infield,
gloving the ball on the short hop and flipping to second
to turn two, and before we each took turns in the cage
with beat-up foam-insulated helmets tamping down the chatter,
we'd sit in a circle of folding chairs to drink lukewarm coffee
under fluorescent lights as a smoky haze churned around us
with nowhere to go. Al-Anon. Alateen. Alcoholics Anonymous.
Crop dusters sprayed sulfur over the vineyards beyond the hospital,
with contrails of pesticide fading away as if whispering secrets
into the earth. I read once that crops were treated with sulfur
in Sumer, 4,500 years ago, that gladiators applied it to their wounds.
And I told no one this, but I was beginning to believe that life
depends on the study of pain, and the management of pain.

The meetings repeated themselves week after week, one month
to another, with someone clearing their throat before reciting
their name aloud, another crying as the rest of us stared
into our empty hands, or into the empty hands of those
seated around us. Their voices gone flat with the telling.
The rest of us suspended in ovals of coffee, framed
by Styrofoam. When it was my turn, I didn't tell the story
of the drive to baseball practice, summers earlier,
near dusk, two six-packs in, his eyelids too heavy
as he tried to focus on the rolling hills of Madera County,
twenty minutes from town, a landscape of dead grass
as far as the eye could see. How quietly tragic it was.
And I didn't share how he implored me to sing,

the windows down and the July heat pouring over us,
the steering wheel floating loose in his hands, a broken
compass without its arrow, his head swaying, slumping
as if everything that had happened in his life now
gathered at the front of his mind, the weight of it
too much to lift anymore, his hair turned silver
decades too soon, and how I sang that day
with my horrible broken little voice, a 12-year-old
who was afraid to speak, a boy who stammered
with words jumbled in his mouth, but still, I sang—

> Slip slidin' away
> Slip slidin' away

And if this were simply a poem, I might end it there—
in that hollow of the road where the sorrow is, even now,
the two of us driving with my sad little voice trailing
from the open window and unraveling in the summer air.
But this is the real world, and as much as he thought
baseball a useless sport, lacking anything that might
stir the intellect, he loved me, even if he didn't understand me,
and I think that's partly the reason he quit drinking, why
he seemed to wake up after more than a decade
of spinning into that void we all carry within.
In the next few years, he taught himself flamenco
and earned his black belt and took up skydiving and
learned how to type and he studied Spanish
and Vietnamese and French and Thai and Swahili
and Arabic and Khmer and Russian and Laotian
and, my god, that blurry haze in his eyes was gone,
and he was sober and he was himself for the rest of his days.

HOW IT WORKS

Phil Levine said, *If you want people to experience loss,*
you have to first give them something to love—

and then take it away. That was in the '90s,
in the San Joaquin Valley, at the bottom

of a dead sea. Maybe I wrote it down,
maybe I didn't. What's important now,

what I've learned most in the time since—
is to fall in love with the small things,

quiet moments, the gestures of strangers
wiping sweat from a brow, a woman lifting

a child to her hip as she hums a few bars
of wordless music, or the way the light moves

through a green century of trees, that story
the rain recites on a corrugated roof.

I can still smell the solvents and abrasives
from the hospital, picture the fluorescent corridors

leading to conversations on radiation and chemo,
the doctors who stare into their own hands

as they offer up the month and season when it all
goes under, as it is with the dead, how they rise

from their bodies and pull their entire lives with them—
mountains, oceans, whole continents, geologic eras,

the deep history of every living being on the planet.
As it's been for me, too, here in the wake

of my own love's crossing. Maybe that's how it works.
I don't know. But that's how it feels. The cities

crumbling in slow motion around me. People's lives
doing the same. Wednesday afternoon. Thursday morning.

Every singing little bird. Every blade of grass. Every
cigarette butt still smoking on the curb. Even that lady's hat

I once saw hovering on the breeze several stories high,
and all of our astonished faces thinking of loved ones

dancing up there, spinning in slow circles. Even that.
All of it pulled into oblivion by the journey of the dead.

SOMEONE TELLS ME THAT DAVID BOWIE HAS DIED.

Of course, David Bowie is always dying.
Song by song, dying. And something about that
places him outside of time. Alive. Singing.
Otherworldly, David Bowie. Celestial traveler.
Bowie spinning through the vinyl darkness
as the Earth spins toward the next millennium,
or maybe toward the last day of our own lives.
The memorials afterward. His music
playing in the heads of those passing by.
Music that recognizes the finite
within the infinite. The you. The me.
The world we have come to love
but does not love us in return.

Someone tells me that the world is dying.
The world is always dying, only this time
it isn't a story, or a failure of the imagination.
The world is dying and it's a Tuesday.
The winged creatures are still flying.
The angry and the sick and the confused
and the beautiful and the kind and the lost
continue in their myriad ways to sing
into a wound so vast some call it a cathedral,
some call it a god, some call it their one precious life.

AN EDUCATION

When I was 5, I ran through the fog of the Visalia Cemetery
calling out the names of my friends as they disappeared
before me, like a featherless bird crying out among the dead,
with no idea that my Uncle Paul, who taught me all I knew
about being a man up to that point, who gave me an alias, *Rinski*—
that he would die on my 31st birthday, with all those broken years
finally taking him down, and that he'd be buried in Section H,
Block 03, Grave 9-1, in plain view of our apartment windows
overlooking the chiseled headstones and skeletal figures
of live oaks stripped of their leaves by winter. Uncle Paul
sometimes loaded the bed of his truck with oranges
stolen from the groves beyond Fresno, and he'd drink
on a shady corner lot while I hawked the merchandise,
jacking up the price as only a small child can. He'd spent
five years in prison for printing fraudulent checks, and later
turned state's evidence when he was on a hit list and wanted
by the Cosa Nostra of California, 11 other names
already crossed out by then, and the U.S. Marshals
placed him under the Witness Protection Program
in the late 1970s, though they never knew he robbed
a liquor store en route to Pennsylvania. He had a tattoo
of my Aunt Karen's name stitched into his forearm
and he slept with a snub-nosed revolver under his pillow.
If his life were a film, it might end aboard a naval ship
off the coast of Vietnam, the anchors of that tattoo
still glowing on his arm as he stepped off the gunwale
as if walking back to San Francisco—that slow motion

falling of his, the decades swirling through his hair.
But for me, it's his return at the death of Disco,
when I was 12. I challenged him to a race I knew I'd win.
375' of gravel drive in Madera, California. To the road
and back. I was a short, scrawny kid, maybe 80 pounds,
at best, and Uncle Paul, he was an old man to me then,
wearing jeans and cowboy boots and his signature grin,
and I can see the two of us poised at the starting line,
when he drops the grin to give me a quick look, then—
only the chipped crunch of boot soles on gravel,
my breathing, my heart pounding in my chest,
and Uncle Paul, my god, so far ahead of me,
running hard, never breaking stride, never looking back.

COCONUT OIL

I don't recall the PA's name, but she recommended
coconut oil as a lubricant, saying, *Sure, the literature*
leans towards water-based lubes, but you can find this
anywhere, any grocery will carry it, and it's a natural
moisturizer, easy enough to clean from the sheets.
And so when I discover a jar in the house years later,
I unscrew the metal lid, close my eyes, and breathe in
a series of moments from a springtime made of
fog and confusion, sunlight and surprise. Chemo
treatments. A trip to Hawai'i. The breakers rolling in
just outside our bedroom window. The night's perfume
carried over the Pacific and reminding us of our time
in Japan, Thailand before that, before the cancer,
when the future lay wide-open. Ilyse
cupped my hips with the soft pads of her hands,
using them as a brake at the iliac crest while coconut
sugared the room with its fragrance. She eased me
down inside of her, pressing back when the raw pain
furled across her brow, crimped her mouth, her
palm heels nearly pushing me out as I couldn't help
but think of the tumors in her bones, spreading
from sternum to vertebrae and then scaling
the ladder of the spine in both directions, so
insidious, so cruel, that cancer revealing itself
by fracturing two of the bones in the middle
of her back a couple of years before, and how,
afterward, I thought it my fault, that I'd done this

without realizing the danger inside of her, on a sunlit
afternoon shared in a tangle of salt and muscle,
our limbs half on half off the bed, the mattress
stripped of its sheets and Ilyse spurring me
harder, harder, so that even now I remember it
at the snap of a finger, and that familiar regret
returns, lingers. And so I close my eyes
and breathe in coconut until the electricity shifts
its current, blue and crackling, the calendar flipping
through months, seasons of our maroon sheets
sliding off the bed, the candle's bright tongue
rising in light as she guides me down, slow,
all of it so tenuous and fragile, on the cusp
of pain, until the oils begin to soften and glide
and her body, easing now, gives way to the smooth
motion of flesh, the two of us made one again,
made strange and new and ancient and beautiful.

1:41

She often sculpted the air with her hands as she spoke,
gesturing the world into being, and I'm reminded of this
as I restart the video so that I might be with her again,
the daylight flooding in through the window behind her
a day I can't place on a calendar, though it's summer,
2016, and in a moment she's going to say, *Oh, how fun,*
as she opens a package filled with tiny prayer bowls,
showing me how she'll hide away messages in each
before shipping them to loved ones around the globe.
In a few seconds, she'll blow a kiss to me and we'll say
I love you before she follows with *Later, maybe we can…*
and I'll never hear the completion of that thought—
I'm left with this 1-minute, 41-second video, this slipping
into the past, the 2020s a blurring of images and voices
that fade as soon as she describes the biplanar wings
of a dragonfly she's conjured from the empty air, jeweled
in its beauty, delicate, its tremulous body waiting for her
to breathe the concept of flight that makes it so.
To do this, her left hand is laid open as her right
caresses the air in a motion that shapes the life-form
being awakened there, flower by lizard by bird, a sweet
kind of magic from within the domain of the imagination.
Petals unfurl their velvet tongues at her lightest touch.
A cat's tail curls its subtle questions into the languid air.
Birds sing their way closer to me, whether anyone
can hear them or not, while the panting lizards

cool themselves in the shadows. I move the cursor.
Press *play* again. If only to hear Ilyse talk about pleasure,
to hear her say, *It's true, I get so much joy in doing this*, and
to linger with her there, in that brief suspension—
her head tilting as if sunlight were pouring into her
while she holds an invisible prayer in her fingertips
that she will soon place within the bowl of her hand.

IN THE RECOVERY ROOM

Hush baby, come to papa, let me hold you

through night's broken circuitry, chromatic
and strafed blue with current.
                              —LYNDA HULL

Inside of me the entire state of California.
Fresno. Madera. Visalia. The hardpan

of the valley floor. The year 1970. 2015. 1984.
Liquor stores. Laundromats. Swimming pools.

Zapp's Park and the Cadillac Club—where I almost
blew out the house speakers with an overdriven bass

back in the day. Versions and variations on these,
all inside of me. And TK, shirtless, barefoot, 180 lbs

of meth-muscle and anger. That boxing ring
in his apartment. The drugs he sold in the kitchen.

And there's my sister, too, her car flipped upside down,
sliding on the rooftop at 70 mph into the olive groves,

the telephone pole that didn't kill her. And my cousin
saying, *Hell yeah, I would've been right there with them,*

if I could've. You kidding me? Carry the flag on the 6ᵗʰ?
Goddamn beautiful if you ask me. But nobody's asking,

and I have to check my own part in all of this, the way
I don't say a thing as he slurs the night air with obscenities—

                                        —and every word of it
a prelude to *All these fuckers can either love it or leave it.*

And the irony is lost on him. He just stares
at the worn expression on my face as he talks on,

as I spit onto the grass and shake my head, knowing
my father would've set him straight, something quick,

in a manner that would have forged respect between them.
But I don't have that in me. I study the pollution

of light. The dim stars trying to break through. All of this
in my head, inside of me, where I stand next to versions

of myself and try to make sense of them all. My grandmother,
frail and skeletal in her hospital bed, squeezing my hand, saying

You can do anything, with such earnest conviction I might
almost believe it myself. And then my father, embracing me

as I graduated from college, saying, *I didn't think*
you could do it. And knowing why he said it—because

nobody had. Life swung sideways on everybody
and who had ever seen a dream all the way through?

Yosemite overlooked us. Its icebound summits
promised beauty—but were often a tank of gas too far.

Like the time I drove halfway to San Francisco
to hear Allen Ginsberg read, my radiator steaming

as I pulled off into the dust and heat near Los Banos,
only two hours from Ginsberg with a gas tank sloshing

barely enough to get back to Fresno, to my good friends,
and a portion of love on planet Earth. I pondered

the burnt hills of the Coast Range mountains,
realizing I might never be in the same room

with Octavio Paz or Gwendolyn Brooks,
that the transcendent was often a gas tank away,

and that I'd have to get back in that Ford Galaxy,
slide the selector lever to D, and drive home. The thing is—

I was wrong about the word *beauty*. I had no idea
how deep the word *love* is rooted within us. Or *perseverance*.

How they braid themselves together. Or what it takes
to see a thing to its end. Maybe that's why Uncle Paul said—

Shhhh. Listen to that, in the recovery room, with his head
propped on pillows at the St. Agnes Medical Center. He pointed

to his chest, now a surgeon's work site, and as I leaned in—
there it was—that faint *tick tick tick* of the metal valve,

and he smiled then, nodding his head, saying, *Rinksi—*
All we ever need is a second chance. Remember that.

And I don't know how to make sense of it all.
The second chances. The no chances. The inheritance

of anger, pain, loss, regret. History. The ocean rolls in
on the evening tide, with a cold moon lifting the water

higher. And here we are just standing out in the yard,
the living among the dead, with my cousin still fuming

and unable to grasp that we're a family, we are all one big family,
somehow standing together and alone all at once, listening

to the language of branches and leaves, the wind in the trees,
police sirens off in the distance, the television glowing

blue in the house with footage of the Capitol under siege.

THE SWEETEST WAY TO DROWN

In the pool, two lovers float on inflatable rafts
as if still in bed from the night before, oblivious
to everything around them. And I am only nine,
but even I know when a promise is being made,
a bond that will carry them through the decades
ahead, lean times when welding and tending bar
won't always be enough, and later, too, when a surgeon
wires his heart back together, and when the car crash
shatters vertebrae in her neck. How cautious and tender
they'll be in the shower then, tracing the sutured furrow
that holds him together before guiding liquid soap
between the bars of the halo and down through
the auburn channels of her hair. These things
we can share. What it's like to watch your parents
fall in love. As they did poolside that summer's day.
Their friends drinking since noon and laughing
in the grass by the smoking grill, hard liquor
poured into tumblers of ice as they told stories
about hospitals and jail and weekends and work,
and mostly their stories were just about being
alive in times like these. And that's when Old Man
Kelman, drunk as usual and slurring about his service
on the HMS Hood, leaned over with his dead eyes
and his dead breath to startle me, then turned away
just as my heels caught the concrete lip of the pool
and I wheeled backwards through the afternoon light—
falling wordless through the ether, a frightened little boy

who didn't know how to swim, though the water
gathered me in its blue embrace, otherworldly,
cold and clear, spangled with the American Bicentennial
that would cast fireworks over Fresno that night.
And in that moment, I couldn't see the rescue coming—
my Uncle Paul, fully-dressed, diving headfirst into the air
at the far end of the pool. I simply watched the number 9
rise higher and higher as I sank towards my own shadow,
which lay on the bottom alongside the shadows cast down
by my mother and the man who would become my father.
And I didn't panic as I sank. My thoughts seemed to mirror
the water. That clarity. I remember it well. It was all so tranquil.
I miss it still. The two lovers drifting side by side, their silhouettes
merging into one. And I held my breath for as long as I could.
And I watched the two of them as they disappeared into the sun.

EXIT INTERVIEW WITH GOD

After we're dead, we're told to wait in old photographs
until it's our time in the queue to sit down with god
and have a good long talk about the ways of the world,
the path we made through it, our attempts to construct
a life that could weather the years allotted to us.

Until then, we remain in monochrome, here in these prints
that expand dimensionally to allow us to wander and dwell
in rooms and fields we no longer fully inhabit, recalling
the hues of green in early May, the rust of an autumn
long since faded into shades of wet aluminum, slate.

It is a state of being framed in silence, though we manage
to communicate as best we can—tracing the figures
of letters through the morning frost on blades of grass,
or simply leaning our heads in the direction
of our thoughts, as shadows also do.

I prefer the park bench beside the lake, the tall trees
listing in a breeze that cannot be felt, as if the world
were a boat endlessly rocking, with birds in silhouette
flying low over the water, their thoughts repeated
as I must be to them, a lone figure, seated, turned upside down.

MARRIAGE

It's been 1,670 days since that Tuesday
in September. That last kiss. That last
breath. There's no changing the facts.
Or the simple truth each day brings. All that is
and all that will never be. I know some say
Til death do us part, but that's not how
the human body works. Or the love
housed within the body. Or how
each of us must learn to live with our dead.
I close my eyes and let the coiled springs
lift me toward the sky. On most nights
Ilyse visits me in my sleep, whispers
another variation on the wild delight
of wild things, her fingers brushing
through my hair as she curls in close
and we drift the blue hours toward dawn.
Is it true that a mattress doubles in weight
over a decade? That jasmine relaxes the body,
heightens desire, and has been used to treat cancer?
In the mornings, I wake to the sweetness of it,
those blossoms just outside our bedroom window.
I listen to her bare feet on the wooden floors.
Water in the kettle, making tea. That high soprano
transforming into steam, vanishing into air.

KISSING

The long afternoon has drugged us.
We melt into one another with our arms
draped over shoulders and hips, eyes closed,
our mouths in a chorus of vowels even the birds
strain to hear. And it's impossible to tell the living
from the dead. The way we entangle ourselves,
nuzzling and burrowing while light and shadow
map the curving geography of our bodies. It is all
so tender. Even the moon floats above, sleeping
alongside us.
        I wake to whisper drowsy,
close, my tongue made of sugar, saying
Ilyse, just imagine, all of this, all of it is ours—
the trembling of the air, the moon and the wind
that carries it across the sky, the two of us, kissing,
for as long as the leaf-green candles in the trees, astonished
by our presence, might burn their way through the onset of dusk.

THE EVERGREEN WORLD

2014

My father stands in the eucalyptus shade
alongside his friends in the French Club
as they play pétanque, shouting, *Carreau, carreau,*
while he soaks it all in, not the sport itself
but the language, its nuance and energy,
its vowels fusing together, each accented
syllable lifting words into bright sentences
that please the ear and transform the city
around him, every bird and leaf and flower,
every cloud rolling by, even his own hands,
the weight of the boule cupped in his palms,
the pendulum of his arm sweeping through
the ether, and that trajectory the mind maps
mid-flight, the outcome already made clear.

1986

My brother and I dropped acid hours ago,
and the Earth has tilted on its axis beneath us.
We're shooting hoops at the playground
in the moon-shaped night, the basketball
spinning in a geometry of tracers the mind
lays in a series of transparencies over the court,
the molecules our guide, electric and wavering,
the globe falling through net—*swoosh, swoosh,*
the trees around us stupefied into silence
as we stand at the top of the key, knees bent

like springs, fingertips launching each flight
as a voice from beyond our sight says, *Damn*
those white boys can shoot, though by morning
the world as we know it will be lost in fog.

     Tonight
Ilyse holds my hand and pulls me forward
into the darkness, which is lovely and deep.
We talk about the architecture of loss, that
mourning of loved ones as years pass on,
the accrual of pain and suffering that makes it so,
and I share how tired I am of the pairing of love
with the travail that follows, all that beautiful ruin
we're taught to pour into the word *grief,* as if
that's the proof we have a human heart
beating within us. No. Tragedy isn't
a certain barometer of the profound.
Instead, I ask if anyone knows how to live
with the dead, how to visit them, and she says
Of course. Just close your eyes. You do it all the time.

THE FORGETTING

Life today will be tomorrow's dream;
a picture painted by the light between
———BRIAN VOIGHT

The cathedral bells of St. Mark's are still ringing
when the Adriatic floods the square with bathers,
splashing and laughing and shivering on a grey afternoon
in human history. The bathers can hardly touch their toes
to the sidewalks of lower Manhattan, too, though the tide
rises higher, story by story, the lower half of Florida
now an underwater shelf of complicated reefwork,
a diver's vast and haunted trove, and above
these vaults—swimmers paddling their way through
memory, anecdote, grand old stories they repeat
to one another with voices growing more circumspect
over the years, the young ones beginning to question
how plausible the terrain of legend might be, the word
plausible a kind of vessel deriving its buoyancy
from the verb *to pause*, as the swimming world must
when the lightless cities turn to shadow and silence
in the hard currents below, the stone monuments gone
speechless in the pitch-black cold, where deepwater fish
gather in their legions to hear what the old gods might say.

THE SUBCONSCIOUS

i. The Lightkeeper of Serifos

The old ship drifts on its mooring lines
in the air over the island, its wooden hull
listing in the breeze to port. On a balcony
carved from stone, I've waited for these sailors
to cast their ropes over the gunwale and rappel
onto the rooftops and into the streets of Chora,
this mountaintop village emptied-out, turned silent
by the onset of winter. I'm here to welcome them
with bottles of wine, loaves of bread, a pot of lemon
chicken soup. If only they might bring word of loved ones
long gone. And if they trust me enough, I'll promise to deliver
the wooden spoons they've carved for those they love, those
who have faded into the years separating them, the way each wave,
once lifting the boat, slides downward, rolls on, never to return.

ii. Sailfish

Maybe I'm the lighthouse and you're the ship
lost at sea. Or maybe you're the prow in the foam
and I'm the anchor sinking into the cold fathoms.
It could be I'm the one climbing into the crow's nest
and you're the bright wind billowing the sails.
I think we might be sailing through an ocean of souls,
lost in a storm, lost in the waves, lost the way lovers

scan the horizon at the break of dawn, at the blue
falling of night. Sailfish guiding us on. Whales
sounding our cries in the dark. The waters
glowing around us, that we might see one another
across the years that mark the divide between
the living and the dead, that we might become
more and more of our own nature, phosphorescent
and shining, turning to shadow. The ocean calming
to silver at the rising of the moon. Sailfish breach
the surface, and our own bodies repeat the motion
until we are sailfish all, our wings unfurled and rippling,
our metallic bodies launched into the unknown
over and over until we finally get it right, our wings
shivering in the uplift, that propulsion into flights
from which we will never return.

iii. Waterspouts

They begin as oval shadows on the surface
with a twist of air, an idea forming beneath a cloud,
a vortex spinning upon itself then rising in a column
until this temporary pipeline connects one world to another—
as the kingdom of fish is transported into the atmosphere
from the epipelagic zone, that sunlit layer of the ocean
from which the spout lifts plankton, anchovies, herring,
jellyfish spiraling upward into the unknown, hundreds
of feet high, and just as quickly as the bridge was built
it spins itself out, the idea realized, the jellyfish floating
on the breeze, their tentacles like ropes given slack,
their bodies drifting across the sky, translucent as silk
parachutes, while anchovies and herring fall headlong

like silver darts aimed at the ruckling surface of the water
below, their tiny mouths windblown open as the jellyfish
float on, at peace with the fact they might never return.

iv. Bathysphere

Tethered to a braided steel cable, the bathysphere descends
layer by layer through the water column, from daylight
to twilight to midnight, then deeper, the cable unspooling
as the metal globe withstands each new increment of pressure,
on descent into a bleak and crushing solitude, the abyssal zone,
where the bathysphere passes anglerfish and tripod fish to enter
a space inhabited by brittle stars and rattail fish, the occasional
Greenland shark, and, deeper still, down into the great rifts
and trenches, to a zone of sea worms and the only fish known
to survive such extremity, pearlfish and snailfish, grenadiers
of the hadal zone, cusk eels hunting in the landscape of Hades,
where the dead spiral down in a steady rain of fuel for the blind
engines of hunger, while a cone of light illuminates the silt
and murk, though what gnaws through the braided steel tether,
shaking the vessel and snapping that connection to the sunlit world
remains a mystery. There is only the bottom of the ocean to call home
now, a bathysphere seeding itself beneath a layer of marine snow,
until, geminated, the metal casing splits open, and a strange stalk
sprouts upward from it with a bioluminescent bulb at its tip,
charged electric, as fish and sea worms gather to witness it
flowering open, petal by petal, a small star at the bottom
of the ocean, shining from a vessel that will never return.

PAPER LANTERNS

We lift our hands into the banded light at dusk
and let go, as each lantern wobbles on the air

before the invisible carries it into the heliotrope
of twilight. It is something to see, this quiet fleet

of prayer rising into darkness. And it's not unlike
the weather balloons a man once filled with helium

tethered to a lawn chair, a fragile airship he built
to enter the sublime, ascending into the atmosphere

before floating over the Pacific at 16,000 feet.
In Japan, Yoshikazu Suzuki followed his lead,

departing from Lake Biwa, where I once stood
before the gravestone of Matsuo Bashō, hoping

it might help me in the creation of my own
haibun. I have no way of knowing what

Suzuki may have been thinking—he was last spotted
500 miles out over the ocean, never to be seen again,

though I imagine him still up there, coasting
on the trade winds, witness to the sun and moon,

clouds pluming into great anvil heads of rain, nights
stunned by tree-shaped voltages of lightning.

And just as Suzuki begins to despair of his solitude,
slow-moving flocks of light rise to greet him,

all our earthly prayers sent from the midnight shores
of our lives, and Suzuki, an old man now, drifting

over the curving sphere he knows by heart, cries
into his weathered hands, cries at the sweetness of it all.

SATURDAYS

A waterfall of light pours the afternoon over us
and, my god, how beautiful you are. I could swear
this is the reason why molecules have worked
so hard and for so long to hold me together,
to keep me from turning into petals and wings
and even the dirt tunneling through the cavernous
hunger of worms. It's true. Our lives blur past
in seasons of rain and fog and thunder. We wake
sometimes in the middle of the night with dreams
of such startling clarity, though by morning it's all
vanished into the pillow, into the warm breath
suffusing the bedroom with that lovely heat
we generate within the tiny engines of our bodies.
We are left with only a vague memory of flying
over the curvature of the Earth, over the wavetops
of grain swaying on the prairie, or the rooftops
of cities rising into the clouds as whole families
simply disappear, the wind in our hair blowing
from the cradle to the grave and then turning
the sunset from tangerine to rust as our bodies
transform from fire to ash within the same sky
that new lovers kiss under, rolling in each other's
sweet entangling, their lips and tongues and fingers
discovering the soft vowels of the word *love*,
as if it were brand new, as if it were an invention

of their own making—and of course it is, every time.
It simply is as it always has been. Our lives so brief.
Time sliding over our bodies like water.

— I —

. . . that beautiful alignment of the outside with the inside . . .
EDUARDO C. CORRAL

THE GOODBYE WORLD POEM

In case I haven't said the thing plain—*I love you.*
I hope you know that. I hope you know it deep down
in the very core of your being, where the imprint
of dream is patterned in a calligraphy of slumber,
where the tangle of our hair is a reminder
of salt and wind, that ocean you adored
something we carry within. That's what I believe—
that we carry everything with us when we go,
the way ships list to starboard with flames in the sailcloth
and rigging, then plunge downward and burn their way
into the deep. It's true. Dying is so intimate, luminous,
composed of shadows. Family. Friends. Flowers.
Mere flashes of light. Fragments. And in the hush
and stillness of the body, our lips are so soft,
our eyes deep in the enormous task a lifetime of dreaming
asks of us as the body begins to hum its new vocabulary.
And the ghosts—they visit with loved ones on the porch
when the wind blows through sometimes, chimes
ringing in the trees. This is what I'm thinking about,
my body no longer driven by oxygen or sunlight,
as I make my way to all that is cold and absolute, here
in this slow crossing, this shimmering dusk, this
gathering of souls into the deep shadow of a mountain.
As we all must do. I'm attending to the difficult harvest
of a life, all the emptiness around us, the everything
that continues on, even as my tongue remains wet
with the language of the body. And I can hear the sound

of loved ones in the distance, sonorous and mournful,
their pathos undeniable, and mournful because
called out for love's sake....There is no escaping this pain,
save for a moment of laughter, maybe, the small
sweet gestures we offer each other, the way
we talk with god within the vaulted spaces of the body.
Something like prayer, maybe, something like memory.
The way we understand water, or air, or drowning,
or how the fog rolls deep in the San Joaquin Valley,
or anything at all. And if this were simply a poem,
we might end it here, in the hollow where the sorrow is,
with my sad little voice vanishing in the summer air,
somewhere at the bottom of a dead sea. But this is
the real world, and maybe I've learned something
about what's most important. Maybe I wrote it down,
maybe I didn't. It was something about falling,
I think. Something about the gestures of strangers.
Quiet moments. Small things. Perhaps it's as Levine said—
You have to first give them something to love. A few bars
of wordless music. Blades of grass. Singing
little birds. I don't know. Maybe that's how it works.
The cities are crumbling in slow motion around me.
Wednesday afternoon. Thursday morning.
All of it pulled into oblivion by the journey
of the dead. The you. The me. The finite
within the infinite. Here in this cathedral
some call god, some call their one precious life.
And like a featherless bird crying out among the dead,
I close my eyes and breathe in the current, blue
and crackling, the months and years gliding by,
until the two of us are made one again, made
strange and new and ancient and beautiful

as you sculpt the air with your hands, tilting your head
for the sunlight to pour in, the prayer in your fingertips
placed inside of me, along with the entire state
of California, versions and variations of these, even
the pollution of light, the dim stars breaking through
until I begin to grasp that we're a family, we are all
one big family, and even if I don't know how to swim
the water will gather me in its embrace, the way it is
for us all when we're dead, each a lone figure
turned upside down in a boat endlessly rocking,
where I count the days since that last Tuesday
in September, that last kiss—that last breath—that
high soprano transforming into steam, vanishing
into air. And it's impossible to tell the living
from the dead here. It's all so tender and serene,
even the moon sleeps alongside us. And Ilyse,
all of this is ours—the stupefied eucalyptus,
the trembling air, every bird and leaf and flower,
every cloud rolling by, the very architecture
of loss, and the human heart itself, all of it
so lovely and deep. It's true. Fish gather to hear
what the old gods might say, while lovers glow
all around us, that we might see one another
across the years marking the divide between the living
and the dead, our bodies launching into the unknown
over and over until we finally get it right, our wings
shivering in flight as the invisible carries us
into the heliotrope of twilight. Oh, my love,
it is something to see. Flying over the curvature
of the Earth, over the wavetops swaying
on the prairies, over the rooftops of cities, where
the lips and tongues and fingers of lovers discover

the soft vowels of the word *love*, as it has always been,
with time sliding over us all like water. And, my god,
how beautiful we are in the ruins. How sweet and brave
in the face of disaster. The way we carry everything with us,
my love, the way we carry everything with us when we go.

Please use this link to listen to the album, *American Undertow*—

NOTES

The Dead Guys. This poem is dedicated to Brian Voight (1967–2012), and to all who played in our band through the years—The Dead Guys. He's mentioned in this book as my brother, because that's what he is to me . . . . Sail on, Brother. I look forward to the day I see you again. Until then, may the sun be on its way to greet you . . . . The line "Ghosts? Oh, I've got ghosts" was something Bruce Weigl said as he and I did a call and response reading at the Solomon R. Guggenheim Museum in New York, December 5th, 2010.

The Dead Guys. "Drift" was engineered and mastered by Brian Voight in Fresno, 2009. Russell Conrad (vocals); Brian Voight (guitars); Brian Turner (bass); Darren Lowenthal (drums).

Vigil. This poem loosely quotes from "Do not go gentle into that good night" by Dylan Thomas (written in 1947) with the line "There is no dying of the light."

All the Quiet Ruin in Gilbert's Poems. The italicized lines are from Jack Gilbert's poem "The Great Fires" (from *The Great Fires*, Knopf, 1996).

Los Angeles. This poem is for poet Corrinne Clegg Hales, whose voice and friendship guides me still, so that I might write my way further into the difficult, beautiful world we live in.

How It Works. The lines ". . . hums a few bars / of wordless music..." is patched together from Philip Levine's poem, "The Music of Time" (*News of the World*, Alfred A. Knopf, 2009). With gratitude to Jehanne Dubrow for discovering the woman in the hat, a sight so singular and lyric I can't stop seeing this time and time again.

Someone tells me that David Bowie has died. This poem is dedicated to Stacey Lynn Brown, and to her love of all things Bowie.

In the Recovery Room. The epigraph is from Lynda Hull's poem "Love Song during Riot with Many Voices" (*Star Ledger,* University of Iowa Press, 1990). . . . My Uncle Paul's nickname for me when I was a boy—*Rinski.* To this day I don't know where he came up with it or what it means, and I can ask, but only the wind responds now. It remains endearing, and I only wish he were here to call me by it still. He was the first father-figure in my life, who taught me the value of being self-reliant, as well as serving as a kind of warning—as he wound up turning state's evidence in trial and hiding out under protection in the Witness Security Program after ending up on a hit list with the Cosa Nostra Mafia.

The Forgetting. The epigraph highlights lyrics from the song "Trilogy," written by Brian Voight.

The Subconscious. Section i is a reimagining of "Lightenings viii" from *Seeing Things* by Seamus Heaney (Faber and Faber, 1991).

Paper Lanterns. This poem is dedicated to poet Kwang Ho Lee.

Saturdays. This poem ends on a variation of a line from Ilyse Kusnetz's poem, "Scientists Decide Past Events Determined by Future Ones: A Lullaby," (*Angel Bones,* Alice James Books, 2019).

The quote from Eduardo C. Corral comes from a craft talk and collaborative Q&A he did with Traci Brimhall during the Palm Beach Poetry Festival in 2021. His craft talk: *Pouring Language into New Containers: Rethinking the Poetic Line.*

ACKNOWLEDGMENTS

I'm grateful to the editors for believing in this work and for publishing earlier versions of the following:

Poetry at Sangam (January, 2020). The opening epigraph was published as part of the poem, "The Weight," then later as part of a collaboration with Sadek Mohammed, Mujib Mehrdad, and Sholeh Wolpé—a book-length meditation on love and loss called *Four Faces of Loss* (al-Wirsha, Baghdad, 2022).

Academy of American Poets' *Poem-a-Day* (July 23, 2019), guest-edited by Paul Guest. "Thera."

FUSION Magazine (October 2021). "Vigil," "The Dead Guys," and "Someone tells me that David Bowie has died." Versions of these poems were included within a hybrid essay of poetry, creative nonfiction, and music.

The Fresno 15: Creative Writing Marathon (FresnoWriters.com). "Fear" and "The Care Unit Softball Team." In October 2021, I drafted a poem each day (all connected in some way to baseball) for this wonderful project—which raises money to support scholarships for writers in the MFA program at Fresno State, my alma mater. Series curator: Jefferson Beavers.

Book of Matches (Issue 2, 2021). "Coconut Oil."

★

I am *deeply* grateful to Carey Salerno for her belief in me and in the work I do, for her vision and guidance in this project from its earliest stages, and for her care in seeing each thing done right. Thank you to all at Alice James Books—both now and through the years—for your steadfast support of my work and for working so hard to see necessary voices take part in a larger poetic conversation now spanning fifty years. Many thanks to Julia Bouwsma for her fine-tuned attention to every word on the page. I'd also like to thank Anya Backlund and Miyako Hannan at Blue Flower Arts for creating doorways into friendships and experiences that continually change my life for the better. And many thanks to Samar Hammam, at Rocking Chair Books, for that first phone call nearly twenty years ago, and for all the conversations since—your friendship and guidance (and wonderful eye in reading my manuscripts and offering advice) has seen me through the hardest of times.

As these manuscripts appeared, one draft to another, I leaned on the good hearts of these incredible writers and human beings with the hope that they might help the work in this trio of collections shine brighter—Laure-Anne Bosselaar, Stacey Lynn Brown, Patrick Hicks, Lee Herrick, Arthur Kusnetz, June Sylvester Saraceno, and Christy Turner (who each read this work during the most trying of times). Thank you. Thank you. Thank you.

*

The album that accompanies this book (*American Undertow*) was made possible by many kind-hearted souls and talented artists. A gift, each and every one.

As you listen to the album, you'll hear Ilyse Kusnetz singing on "Monochrome" and "Slow 70's Groove."

Brian Voight wrote the song and plays acoustic guitar on "Gasoline Love" and "Wayward Traveler." When I returned to Fresno after my time in the Army, he and I recorded these on acoustic guitars in his apartment, sometime in the spring/ summer of 2005. That's his voice saying, "Just to get the tone, see what we have to adjust and all . . . . One, two, three—go."

Chantal Thompson is featured on this album, singing on 1, 2, 3, 8, 10.

Brian Turner: vocals on most of the songs; bass on tracks 1, 3, 4, 5, 6, 7, 8, 10, 11; guitar on 4, 6, 8, 9, 11.

Benjamin Kramer—bass on tracks 3, 7, 9, 10; string arrangements & programming on 4, 6, 8, 9, 10.

Christian Kiefer: drums on tracks 1, 7, 8, 10; guitars on 1, 7; keyboards on 7.

Bobby Koelble: guitars on tracks 2, 3, 4, 6, 8, 11.

Lee Baggett: guitar on track 11.

Terri Kent: vocals on 4, 11.

T.R. Hummer: saxophone on track 8.

Peter Catapano: drums on track 5.

Steve Woodward: drums on 3, bossa nova drums on 6.

Danny Jordan: saxophone on track 10.

Vocals: Aja Monet 10; Russ Conrad 7; Sarah Cossaboon 8.

All tracks engineered, mixed, and mastered by Benjamin Kramer at 2Pi Creative Studios, Orlando, Florida—except:

Chantal Thompson's vocals were recorded by Jason Mercer at Neptune's Machine, Wolfe Island, Ontario.

T.R. Hummer's saxophone recorded by Todd Giudice at Roots Cellar Recording in Cold Spring, New York.

Terri Kent's vocals were recorded by Michael Cox at Uprise Recording in Sacramento, California.

Russell Conrad's vocals were recorded by Eric Sherbon at Maximus Media, Inc. (with thanks also to Ray Settle).

★

I send my love and gratitude to those mentioned above, and also to Tony Barnstone, Jefferson Beavers, Shannon Beets, Jeff Bell, Kevin Bowen, Seth Brady Tucker, Gayle Brandeis, Doyle Buhler, Camille Dungy, Pablo Cartaya, Matt Cashion, Sophie Cherry, Steven Church, Russell Conrad, Shawn Crouch, Roel Daamen, Rupa DasGupta, Rob Deemer, Kurt & Heidi Erickson, Sarabjeet Garcha, Patsy Garoupa, Alison Granucci, Kelle Groom, Paul Guest, Nathalie Handal, Charles Hanzlicek, Lisa Lee Herrick, Faylita Hicks, Devin High, Garrett Hongo, T.R. Hummer, Ashwani Kumar, Dorianne Laux, Kwang Ho Lee, Rebecca Makkai, Tim Maxwell, Laura McCullough, Katie McDowell, Thomas McGuire, Christopher Merrill, Mujib Merhdad, Dunya Mikhail, Joe Millar, Sadek Mohammed, Peter Mountford, Soheil Najm, Matt O'Donnell, April Ossmann, Oliver de la Paz, Benjamin Percy, Susan Rich, Suzanne Roberts, Jake Runestad, John Schafer, Sean Sexton, Ravi Shankar, Jared Silvia, Krystal Sital, Patricia Smith, Michael Thomas, Chantal Thompson, Bill Tuell, Bruce Weigl, Sholeh Wolpé, Lidia Yuknavitch, and Arianne Zwartjes—thank you for allowing me to be a part of your phenomenal lives. One of my deep regrets is in not adequately expressing how grateful I am to each of you.

To Corrinne Clegg Hales—I was the shy kid at the back of the class with the profound stammer, and I'll always be grateful for your encouragement and for all that you taught me about the art itself. Thank you for your friendship and mentorship over the years, Connie.

To Patrick Hicks—With every draft and revision, you've been there as my first reader. It's been an unspoken thing, a gift of such profound magnitude, and always with a keen eye to the art itself, while—at a deeper level—helping me as I attempt to write my way into the rest of my life.

To Stacey Lynn Brown—Through the highs and lows that years and decades bring, you remain a constant friend through it all. It's been a gift to be a part of your life. Remember—if you find yourself in a bar fight (which I don't recommend), don't worry, I got your back (and I'll hold your drink).

To Benjamin Busch—Thanks for keeping me upright and steady in the low times, man, and for hitting the high notes that remind us all that Rock is not dead.

To June Sylvester Saraceno—Thanks for being the gift of a sister I met late in a life. I'll meet you at the river with Luna and Dene! Thank you for always being there for me.

To Bill and Russ and Skip and Captain—Brothers, I'll see you in the band room when we all meet up with Brian Voight and John Irola one day. Here's raising a glass to The Dead Guys in its many variations—and to each of you.

I send my abiding love to friends and family, loved ones all, both near and far.

★

Ilyse, my love to you, always

RECENT TITLES FROM ALICE JAMES BOOKS

The Wild Delights of Wild Things, Brian Turner

I Am the Most Dangerous Thing, Candace Williams

Burning Like Her Own Planet, Vandana Khanna

Standing in the Forest of Being Alive, Katie Farris

Feast, Ina Cariño

Decade of the Brain: Poems, Janine Joseph

American Treasure, Jill McDonough

We Borrowed Gentleness, J. Estanislao Lopez

Brother Sleep, Aldo Amparán

Sugar Work, Katie Marya

Museum of Objects Burned by the Souls in Purgatory, Jeffrey Thomson

Constellation Route, Matthew Olzmann

How to Not Be Afraid of Everything, Jane Wong

Brocken Spectre, Jacques J. Rancourt

No Ruined Stone, Shara McCallum

The Vault, Andrés Cerpa

White Campion, Donald Revell

Last Days, Tamiko Beyer

If This Is the Age We End Discovery, Rosebud Ben-Oni

Pretty Tripwire, Alessandra Lynch

Inheritance, Taylor Johnson

The Voice of Sheila Chandra, Kazim Ali

Arrow, Sumita Chakraborty

Country, Living, Ira Sadoff

Hot with the Bad Things, Lucia LoTempio

Witch, Philip Matthews

Neck of the Woods, Amy Woolard

Alice James Books is committed to publishing books that matter. The press was founded in 1973 in Boston, Massachusetts to give women access to publishing. As a cooperative, authors performed the day-to-day undertakings of the press. The press continues to expand and grow from its formative roots, guided by its founding values of access, excellence, inclusivity, and collaboration in publishing. Its mission is to publish books that matter and preserve a place of belonging for poets who inspire us. AJB seeks to broaden our collective interpretation of what constitutes the American poetic voice and is dedicated to helping its artists achieve purposeful engagement with broad audiences and communities nationwide. The press was named for Alice James, sister to William and Henry, whose extraordinary gift for writing went unrecognized during her lifetime.

Designed by Alban Fischer

Printed by Sheridan Saline